# MONEY SKILLS EVERY KID NEEDS TO KNOW

A Beginner's Guide to Earning, Saving, Spending,

Sharing & Growing

# CONTENTS

# Chapter 1 — Meet Your Money: A Beginner's Guide to Earning, Saving, Spending, Sharing, and Growing

Money is a tool, not a personality test. It does not know whether you are generous or greedy, brave or shy, lucky or unlucky. It simply follows instructions—yours. For many kids and teens, the first encounter with money is tiny and sudden: a birthday envelope, a few coins from a chore, a digital gift card blinking on a screen. Because the amounts are small, it is tempting to treat money like confetti—toss it in the air and let it vanish. This book treats money differently. It is a beginner's guide to turning cash and coins into choices and confidence.

Think of money as a loop instead of a one-time event. First you earn it. Then you assign it jobs. You protect it so it stays yours. You use it with a clear purpose. You review what happened so the next loop is smarter. The five stations on this loop have simple names: earn, save, spend, share, and grow. As you ride the loop again and again, money stops feeling mysterious and starts feeling manageable. Instead of asking "Where did it all go?" you begin to say "I told it where to go."

Earning is the beginning of choice. When you are young, your earnings will be small and supervised, and that is perfect for learning. Safety and local rules matter more than quick cash, and your well-being is worth more than any job. That said, there are many age-appropriate ways to earn: feeding a neighbor's pet while they are away, watering plants, sorting books, tutoring a younger student in a subject you enjoy, setting up chairs for events, or creating simple crafts for a family market. The job itself teaches punctuality, reliability, and pride. It also teaches a quiet truth that will stay with you: people pay for help that solves their real problems.

Saving is not punishment for wanting things. Saving is choosing to make bigger, better choices later. A simple method is to pay your future self first by moving a slice of new money into a safe place the moment you receive it. Some families like three jars or three digital "buckets" labeled SAVE, SPEND, and SHARE. Others add a fourth word—GROW—when kids are ready to learn about interest. Goals make saving easier because they answer "What is this for?" A near-term goal could be a book series, soccer cleats, or art supplies. A longer-term goal might be a camp fee or a contribution to a class trip. When you write a number, a date, and a reason, your brain gets a map to follow.

Spending is where values show up. Before buying, pause long enough to ask three simple questions. Do I need it? Will I use it often? Will it last? A fourth question lowers pressure: Could I borrow this or buy it second-hand? Wise spending is not about never buying anything fun; it is about noticing the difference between a quick thrill and real usefulness. Ads are designed to make wants feel urgent. Values are designed to make wants wait. One overnight pause reveals a lot. If the desire is still loud tomorrow, consider it. If it has faded to a whisper, you just saved yourself from a forgettable purchase.

Sharing is the part of the loop that surprises people. The first time you give money away and feel bigger instead of smaller, you learn something true: generosity grows the giver. Sharing can be coins in a collection jar, a portion of allowance sent to a cause, or a decision to combine spending money with friends so a classmate can join the same event. You do not need to give in public or give more than you can afford. What matters is choosing a purpose you care about and noticing the lift you feel when your money carries kindness farther than your pockets.

Growing money is where time does quiet magic. If a bank or credit union pays interest, they are paying you rent for letting your money live with them. Over long stretches, interest can be added to your original money and start earning its own interest. This is called compounding. Compounding's best friend is time; the sooner you begin, the more time your money has to grow. There are other ways to try to grow money in the world beyond savings accounts, but those paths include risk as well as reward. Kids and teens should explore these ideas with adults who can explain local rules and help set safe boundaries. The core principle will stay clear: start safe, start small, and understand what you are doing before you do more.

Safety is not only about banks and math; it is about people, devices, and decisions. Keep cash and cards somewhere that is not easy for strangers to reach. Protect your PINs and passwords the way you protect your house keys. Be cautious with messages that promise prizes or ask for codes, and ask a trusted adult whenever something financial feels rushed or secret. Your privacy has value. You do not need to say yes to every form that asks for your address or to every app that wants your location. Strong habits protect your money before you even touch it.

Feelings matter in money. Excitement, boredom, envy, fear—all can push decisions. When you name the feeling—"I'm buying this because I want to fit in," or "I'm skipping this because big crowds make me tired"—you turn fog into a map. Families can help by making money talk normal rather than secret. Discuss trade-offs in the grocery aisle, compare unit prices, and laugh together when you catch a silly ad trying to sell the same thing with a louder voice. The more comfortable you are with honest talk, the easier it is to ask questions and learn.

A budget is a plan for the next loop of your money. For teens it might include expected earnings, a target for saving, a small amount you intend to share, and what you think you will spend on snacks, transport, school activities, or hobbies. A good budget is not a handcuff; it is a guide you redraw as you learn. At the end of a week or a month, look back and ask what surprised you. If your plan and reality differed, how will you adjust? You are not grading yourself. You are upgrading yourself.

Tracking is like keeping a travel journal for your money. If you write down where your money went—even for a two-week experiment—you will discover patterns hidden in ordinary days. Perhaps you spent more on small treats than you guessed, or perhaps you saved more than you remembered because you kept choosing to bring water from home. Tracking is not meant to shame you. It is meant to give you a clearer picture so you can choose your next step with open eyes.

The story of money is also the story of time. A purchase steals time or gives it back. An item that breaks quickly steals not only the dollars you paid but the minutes you will spend replacing it. A skill that lets you fix, cook, or create gives you time later because you won't need to wait for someone else. Each choice either crowds your future or clears it. This is why values matter. When you decide what kind of person you are becoming—helpful, curious, dependable—you teach your money how to behave.

Imagine two friends, Maya and Leo. They both receive $10 a week from odd jobs. Maya spends hers quickly on small treats that are fun in the moment but forgettable. Leo follows the loop. He pays his future self first—$4 into savings, $1 into sharing—and keeps $5 for spending. After eight weeks Maya wonders where her money went. Leo buys a used science kit he has wanted for months and still has a small cushion left. Their choices are not about who is smarter or nicer. They are about habit and time.

Now imagine a little risk lesson. Leo hears about a "can't-lose" online scheme promising to double any money sent in. He pauses, shows it to his parent, and together they spot the warning signs: no clear company address, rushed language, demands for gift card codes. Leo keeps his money, reports the scam, and learns a lasting skill: when money feels rushed or secret, slow down and verify. The best "deal" is the one that is still a good idea after a night of sleep.

Here is a small script you can borrow the next time a want feels urgent: "I'm excited about this. I'll write down the price, the date, and the reason, and I'll check tomorrow. If it still matters, I'll see whether it fits my plan." You are not telling yourself "never." You are telling yourself "not yet," which is a superpower in a world that shouts "now."

Compounding is easier to understand with a picture in words. Suppose you place $5 every week into a savings account. After ten weeks you have $50 plus a little interest. After fifty weeks you have $250 plus more interest. The interest looks tiny at first, almost invisible. But interest is patient; it never asks for weekends off. Over years it grows from a quiet whisper into a steady voice. Starting early lets time be on your team.

Inflation is the opposite direction. Prices rise slowly over time, which means yesterday's dollar buys a little less today. That is why it helps to keep long-term savings in places that can at least try to keep pace and to revisit prices on your goals. The camp fee that was $180 last year might be $190 this year. Knowledge prepares you, not scares you.

Another way to grow is by growing yourself. When you learn a skill—coding a small website for a family friend, baking bread that customers pre-order at a school sale, repairing squeaky bike brakes—you increase your "earning engine." A skill lasts longer than a toy and can be used again and again. The money you make from using a skill can be saved, shared, or reinvested to improve the skill. This is how small ventures begin: with service, not with shortcuts.

All along the loop, your digital life matters. Use strong, unique passwords and keep your devices locked. Be careful with photos of money and purchases online; scammers watch for clues. Check transactions regularly and speak up if something looks wrong. Adults make mistakes with money; teens do too. What matters is catching errors early and learning from them.

Family conversations are the secret fuel of good money habits. Ask your caregivers how they make choices at the store. Offer to read a receipt and find unit prices. Share your goals and ask for advice on timelines. If your family uses allowances or earnings, learn the system and suggest improvements that make sense to you. Money talk does not have to be heavy. It can be curious, practical, even funny.

At the end of each loop, do a tiny review. What did I earn? What jobs did I give my money? What felt wise? What would I change next time? Write two sentences in your money journal and close it. Those sentences, repeated across months, will build a story of growth that is bigger than any one purchase.

Finally, remember that money is not a scoreboard for your worth. It is a toolbox. Some months the tools are many; some months they are few. What matters is using the tools you have to build the life you want and to help others when you can. Earn with safety and pride. Save with purpose. Spend with awareness. Share with heart. Grow with patience and understanding. Each lap around the loop teaches a lesson the next lap will use. That is how money becomes a friend.

## Chapter 2 — How Money Flows: Income, Expenses, and Cashflow

Cashflow is the rhythm of your financial life—the timing of money in and the timing of money out. Because teens often earn in bursts and spend in drips, your rhythm will feel uneven at first. That is normal. Your job is to make the rhythm visible so you can steer it. Begin by writing a one-page plan for the next four weeks. At the top, list what money you expect to arrive, from allowance to babysitting to tournament refereeing. On the left, list the expenses you control—snacks, transport, outings, school events, gifts, hobbies—and include saving and giving as planned "expenses." On the right, copy dates onto a calendar so the timing is clear. Five dollars arriving a week after the field trip cannot pay for the bus you needed yesterday.

Now set your most important rule: the moment new money arrives, split it according to your plan. Moving a slice into savings and another slice into giving takes seconds and prevents "it all evaporated" syndrome. You can use labeled envelopes, three jars, or app buckets; what matters is the separation. Next, decide which expenses are fixed and which are flexible. Fixed costs repeat and are hard to avoid—club dues, a monthly app you truly need, the bus for practice. Flexible costs respond to your decisions—cafés, upgrades, game purchases, random extra snacks. As a beginner, try to keep fixed costs light so surprises do not wreck your plan.

Cashflow gains power when you review it weekly. Choose a small ritual—Friday evenings for ten minutes, or Sunday after lunch—and look at three questions. What came in? What went out? What needs moving? Shifting five dollars from "fun" to "savings" early in the month is easier than scrambling at the end. Add a cushion line to your plan—money that has no job but "absorb surprises." A small cushion keeps broken earbuds or a sudden class poster from breaking your flow.

Irregular income requires a different mindset than a salary. Treat big bursts like a farmer treats harvest: you store most of it for later seasons. If you earn forty dollars one weekend, it may need to cover three weekends of small spending. The best way to make this work is to pay yourself a steady "weekly allowance" out of your own stored cash. In effect, you become your own employer, smoothing the bumps so daily life stays predictable. Your stored cash is not just savings; part of it is future spending given out on schedule.

Put your calendar to work. Every expected cost—tournament travel, friend's birthday, school dance ticket—goes onto the date it will happen. If it repeats, like monthly membership, add it to the first day of every month. When you turn to a new week, you will see the costs waiting for you, not be surprised by them. This is how adults protect their peace; it also works for teens. A calendar is a cashflow instrument as much as a planner.

Use numbers to check feelings. If you feel broke, write the numbers; you may discover you are anxious but not actually out of money. If you feel rich after a cash burst, write the numbers; you may find only a fraction is free to spend. Numbers do not remove feelings, but they give feelings something useful to hold. Over time you will learn your personal rhythm—when temptation hits, when you splurge, when you save easily—and you can build guardrails around the wobbly parts.

Consider running a two-week experiment called "spend what's planned." Before the week begins, assign a simple dollar amount for flexible categories—maybe eight dollars for snacks, six for small outings, four for hobbies. As the week passes, spend only from those amounts. When a category empties, you pause rather than borrow from the future. At the end, notice how it felt. If the amounts were too tight, increase them a little; if they were too loose, let savings climb. The point is not punishment. The point is proving that a plan you design beats a plan designed by impulse.

Cashflow also lives in small daily decisions. Bringing a water bottle avoids two to four dollars of drinks each week. Learning to make basic breakfasts at home saves five to ten a weekend. Choosing library holds over one-click ebook purchases rescues larger amounts than you expect. None of these choices ask you to be joyless; they ask you to be intentional. When you choose on purpose, you feel more free, not less.

Finally, protect your cashflow from leaks you cannot see at first. Subscriptions that restart after a free trial will quietly nibble at your plan. In-app purchases, especially in games, tend to arrive as "just ninety-nine cents" that add up. Shared rides that seemed cheap at the time may knock your cushion flat. Once a month, print or save your statements and scan for repeating charges. Cancel what no longer serves your values and keep the ones that truly earn their keep. Cashflow is not about saying no forever; it is about saying yes to what matters on time, every time.

## Chapter 3 — Earn Safely and Well: Age — Appropriate Ways to Make Money

Earning is your first laboratory for value. The core lesson is simple: people pay for help that solves their real problems. Think like a helper, not like a hunter of dollars. Start with safety and permission. Follow your family's rules and your community's regulations; work in places where adults can supervise; share your schedule with a caregiver; and carry a phone number you can call if plans change. Safety is the non-negotiable profit.

List common needs in your neighborhood. Pets need feeding and walking when owners travel; plants need water during vacations; younger students need patient tutoring; garages need organizing;

grandparents need help with phone settings; events need setup and cleanup; team parents need an extra driver to pick up supplies; families love pre-ordered baked goods made in clean kitchens under adult oversight. Choose one or two services you can deliver well. Then write a one-paragraph offer that explains what you do, where and when you do it, how much it costs, and how customers pay. Clear offers save awkward conversations and protect both sides.

Price fairly by thinking in projects, not just hours. People value a clean result more than a long timer. If dog-feeding takes fifteen minutes twice a day, quote a simple per-day price that includes a photo update and a note. If tutoring takes forty-five minutes, choose a per-session fee that includes ten minutes of prep. If you bake, calculate your costs—ingredients, labels, boxes—and set a price that covers costs plus a small profit. Keep a page of records so you learn what jobs truly pay after materials and travel.

Deliver more care than promised. Arrive five minutes early. Bring a small notepad and write down special instructions. Send a quick text at the halfway point. Clean the space you used. Thank your customer and ask whether anything could be improved next time. Small professional habits turn first jobs into repeat jobs, and repeat jobs build both income and reputation.

Build a tiny portfolio. Take photos of your organized shelf (with permission), collect two short testimonials from satisfied customers, and keep a list of tasks you've mastered. When you propose new work, show your portfolio on a single printed page or a simple website your family approves. Confidence grows when you can point to results. Never post names, faces, or addresses without consent; respect for privacy is part of being professional.

Know your stop rules. If a situation feels wrong—an adult you do not know asks for a ride, a house feels unsafe, a job shifts far beyond the agreement—you call a caregiver and leave. You do not "power through" red flags. Your safety is worth more than any paycheck. Likewise, know your rest rules. School, sleep, and health come first. Money that costs too much life is expensive indeed.

Finally, treat earning as a class you can ace. After each job, debrief yourself in three lines: what went well, what was hard, what I'll change next time. Adjust your script and your price as you learn. If demand is high, raise quality before price: add a checklist, bring better tools, create a pickup system. Earning well is not a race to charge the most; it is a craft of reliable help. The money follows the care.

## Chapter 4 — Goals that Stick: Turning Wishes into Savings Plans

Wishes whisper; goals speak clearly. To turn a wish into a plan, you need one sentence with a number, a date, and a because. "I'm saving $120 by September 10 because I want a used guitar to practice with the school band." Write it in large letters where you see it daily. Then convert the number into steps you can actually take—ten dollars a week for twelve weeks, or eight dollars plus two dollars matched by a parent who supports the goal. The math is not the hard part. The hard part is remembering the goal when the world is loud. That is why visibility matters.

Design your environment so sticking becomes easier than slipping. Move savings first the moment money arrives; this removes decision fatigue. Keep your goal chart on the door you open most. Put a photo of the guitar, the trip, or the class at the top of your homework folder. Tell one friend and one adult what you are doing so they can cheer you on and ask you about progress. Small public promises help you keep private promises to yourself.

Expect turbulence. A birthday invitation appears, prices change, a ride you expected falls through. When the plan wobbles, adjust the steps, not the dream. You can extend the date, add a tiny side job, sell items you no longer use, or pause a low-value expense for a month. If you fall behind completely, rewrite the one-line goal and begin again. Goals are not all-or-nothing; they are maps you redraw as you learn the landscape.

Create a "sinking fund" for any goal that repeats, like sports fees or trips that happen each year. A sinking fund is a special envelope or app bucket where you store money for a future expense you know is coming. Pay it first. Watching the fund grow removes dread and replaces it with calm preparedness. When the invoice arrives, you simply move money from the fund instead of scrambling.

Keep motivation alive with milestone moments. Every time you cross ten percent of the goal, do something small that supports the goal—watch a tutorial about the skill, clean and prepare the space where the item will live, or write a note thanking your future self for sticking with it. Do not "celebrate" by undoing progress; match the reward to the journey. Your brain needs evidence that the plan is working and that the effort is worth it.

Finally, link your goal to identity. If you see yourself as the kind of person who keeps promises, including money promises to your future self, choices simplify. The treat you skip is not a loss; it is a vote for the person you are becoming. The chart you color is not childish; it is grown-up discipline in friendly ink. Goals that stick do not happen because you are tougher than everyone else. They happen because you rewrote the world around you to make the next right step easy to take and satisfying to see.

## Chapter 5 — Budget Basics You Can Keep

Budgets fail when they are perfect on paper and impossible in life. A teen-friendly budget is small, visual, and flexible. Start with three lines: expected income for the month, planned saving and giving, and categories for spending that reflect your real week—school days, weekends, and hobbies. Give every dollar a job. If you expect $80 to arrive in different bursts, you might plan to save $24, share $8, and spend $48. Within the spending line, split by pattern: transport, snacks, outings, supplies. Keep the entire plan on one page so it lives with you instead of hiding in a file you never open.

Irregular income calls for a zero-based approach. Each time money arrives, assign all of it. Do not "let it sit" in a general pile. Move the saving and sharing slices first, put the planned amounts in their envelopes or app buckets, and leave the rest as flexible spending. When a bucket empties, your decision is to wait, not to borrow from next month. Waiting is a skill. It turns budgets from cages into coaches.

Review weekly, not just monthly. A month is too long to fly blind. Your Friday ten-minute check asks three things: Did money arrive as expected? Did spending match the buckets? What will I change for the next seven days? If transport cost more because of extra rehearsals, move money from a low-value area. If snacks exploded because you were always in a hurry, plan simple grab-and-go food at home. Budgets are not about shame; they are about designing the next week to fit reality.

Use ratios that suit your goals. Many teens start with 70-20-10 for spending-saving-sharing. Others prefer 60-30-10 if they are sprinting toward a big target. The ratio is not a law. It is a lens that reminds you to feed the future and care for others before fun devours everything. As responsibilities grow, your ratio will shift again. A good budget grows up with you.

Add two safety nets. The first is a small cushion line—five to twenty dollars reserved for "life happens." The second is a list of "stop-gap actions" you will use before you ever borrow: cook at home, pause one subscription, ask for a ride swap, or choose a free hangout instead of a paid one. When stress is high, decisions are weak. Prewriting your responses turns emergencies into checklists.

Finally, remember that a budget is permission, not just prevention. It grants you the right to enjoy the money you planned to enjoy without guilt. If your "weekend fun" bucket has eight dollars, use them with a smile. You kept your promises to savings and sharing; you balanced needs with wants. That is not being stingy. That is being the boss of your money instead of its employee.

## Chapter 6 — Spend Wisely: Needs, Wants, and the Total Cost of Use

Spending is where your values and your calendar shake hands. The quickest way to upgrade spending is to upgrade your questions. Instead of "Do I want this?" ask "What job will this item do in my life? How often will it work? How long will it last? What will it cost me per use?" Calculate the total cost of use by adding the price, the accessories it needs, the time to learn it, and the time to maintain it. A durable backpack that survives three school years at $45 costs about $15 per year. A fashionable but fragile pack that fails after one semester costs $30 per semester plus the hassle of replacement. Time is part of price.

Next, learn to compare fairly. Unit price labels in stores reveal the cost per ounce, per liter, or per sheet. Big boxes are not always cheaper; sometimes a smaller package on sale wins because the unit price drops more. Sales themselves can be fog machines. A red tag does not guarantee value if the item solves no problem for you. Put the purchase on trial: What claim is the seller making? What evidence is offered? Who benefits if you rush? Asking for evidence turns you from a follower into a chooser.

Quality leaves clues. Check stitching on clothes, zippers on jackets, the hinge action on cases, the evenness of seams on shoes. Read materials: stainless steel is tough; aluminum is light; wool stays warm when damp; cotton breathes but shrinks; sturdy BPA-free plastics take hits; glass resists odor and scratches but can break. Prefer designs you can repair—replaceable straps, standard batteries, parts you can order. Repairability is a kind of savings account hidden inside an object.

Beware of subscriptions and micro-transactions that slip under your decision radar. A "free" app with a $4.99 monthly upgrade becomes $60 a year; a game with gems and skins can quietly siphon pocket money that never reaches your goals. If you truly value the service, put it in the budget with a start date and an end date, and set a reminder to review it. If you do not, cancel quickly and move on. Every dollar carries an opportunity cost—the next best thing it could have done for you. You want your dollars doing their best jobs, not playing in the corner.

Borrowing, renting, and buying used are smart options, not signs you are poor. Libraries are treasure rooms. Tool libraries, gear swaps, and community buy-nothing groups extend your reach without draining cash. When you do buy used, inspect carefully, test thoroughly, and ask about return options. Many of the most satisfying purchases are pre-owned items chosen with care, because they deliver function without the pain of brand-new prices.

Finally, give yourself a pause button. If the purchase is not urgent, wait twenty-four hours. If it is a bigger purchase, wait a week. Write the item, the price, and the reason on a card. If the desire grows stronger for a clear reason, proceed. If it fades, you learned something without paying. Wise spending is not the absence of fun. It is the presence of meaning. When every purchase lines up with who you are becoming, you feel lighter walking out of the store, not heavier.

# Chapter 7 — Track and Review: Your Money Journal

What you measure, you can improve. A money journal replaces guesswork with evidence. For two to four weeks, write a short entry for each money moment. Include the date, the item, the amount, why you bought it, and how you felt before and after. Add income entries too—where the money came from and how long it took to earn. The journal is not a courtroom; it is a lab notebook. Curiosity works better than judgment.

Patterns will appear. You may discover that after long practices you default to expensive snacks because you did not pack anything.

You may see that café trips are actually friend time in disguise and can be moved to cheaper places without losing joy. You may learn that your "just in case" purchases rarely get used. With patterns in hand, design small experiments. Pack a snack for a week. Make a home-coffee challenge with a friend. Hide the in-game shop behind a screen-time password an adult controls. Record results—money saved, happiness kept—and keep what works.

Use simple totals to learn faster. At week's end, add three numbers: total income, total spending, total saved and shared. Then write three sentences: the smartest dollar I spent, the dollar I would do differently, and the next tweak I will test. This tiny review builds wisdom one paragraph at a time. If you love spreadsheets, track there. If you prefer paper, use a small notebook. Tools matter less than habits.

Capture emotions so you remember the human story behind the math. Were you bored, stressed, celebratory, or tired? Did an ad, a friend's comment, or a deadline push you? What would future you thank past you for doing right now? Over time, the journal will teach you where to put friction (delete saved cards; uninstall a shopping app) and where to remove friction (pre-load the library hold page; keep $2 of bus fare in your case).

Finally, share highlights with a trusted adult or mentor once a month. Teaching someone what you learned locks the lesson in place and opens the door to advice you did not know to ask for. The goal is not perfect records forever; it is a burst of attention that upgrades your instincts. Two focused weeks of tracking each season will do more for your growth than a year of vague guessing. Your journal is a mirror you can carry in your pocket, one that shows you the future you are building today.

## Chapter 8 — Banks and Credit Unions: Accounts, Interest, and Safety

Banks and credit unions are safes that also keep score. They protect money from loss and theft, help you move it where it needs to go, and pay a little interest in certain accounts. With a parent or guardian, explore youth accounts available where you live. Learn the basic vocabulary: deposit means putting money in; withdrawal means taking it out; balance is how much you have right now; a statement is the monthly report card of what moved. Ask whether the institution is covered by a protection program in your country and how interest is calculated and paid. Protection and clarity are why people use banks.

Understand account types. A savings account is built to store money and usually pays interest. It may limit how often you can move funds. A checking or payment account is built to move money—debit card purchases, transfers, paying a bill—but often pays little or no interest. Some youth accounts bundle both functions with parent controls. None of these are magic; they are tools that do what they are designed to do. Keep long-term money where it earns and short-term money where it can move.

Fees are the pebbles in your shoe. Ask which fees apply and how to avoid them: minimum balance fees, out-of-network ATM withdrawals, paper statement charges, or international card fees when you travel. Alerts are your early-warning system. Turn on notifications for low balances and unusual transactions, and read them. When you spot something odd, act fast: freeze the card in the app if your bank allows it and tell a guardian. Speed limits damage.

Security is mostly habit. Use strong, unique passwords and add two-factor authentication when available. Keep your phone locked and log out on shared devices. Never share one-time codes. Be cautious with public Wi-Fi when checking accounts, and use official apps rather than links from messages. Review your statements monthly; the discipline of reading them will teach you more about how you actually use money than any lecture.

Finally, treat your bank like a partner you respect. Read what you sign; ask questions until you understand; keep records of deposits (photos of checks, notes on cash). If you make a mistake—overdraw an account or send money to the wrong place—tell the bank immediately. People on the other side of the counter want to help customers who are honest and quick to act. Banking is not glamorous, but it is one of the quiet superpowers of adult life. Begin now, while the amounts are small, and the habits will be ready when the amounts are larger.

## Chapter 9 — Cards, Wallets, and Digital Payments: Use with Care

Cards and digital wallets are convenient, powerful tools—like power drills for money. Used well, they save time and reduce risk; used carelessly, they can cause expensive mistakes. The first rule is to understand what you are holding. A debit card moves money you already own from your bank account to a store. A prepaid card spends only what you loaded in advance. A credit card—which most teens use only with adult supervision—borrows money you must repay, often with extra cost called interest if you wait. A mobile wallet on a phone does not create new money; it simply stores your card details safely and lets you pay by tapping. Each tool has a place, and none of them replace judgment.

Start with a safe setup. Use a youth or family account that allows adult oversight. Turn on card controls in the bank app: spending alerts, low-balance warnings, and the ability to freeze the card from your phone. Set transaction limits that match your reality. Add a phone passcode and biometrics, and keep devices updated. In your wallet, store just what you need: one card you actually use, a school ID, and a transit pass if required. Leave rarely used cards at home. Memorize your PIN and never share it; a PIN is a house key, not a handshake.

Day-to-day habits protect you more than once-a-year lectures. Keep your card in a consistent place—front right slot, for example—so you notice immediately if it is missing. When paying in person, don't hand your phone or card to strangers; tap yourself. Cover the keypad when entering your PIN. Ask for a printed or digital receipt if the purchase might be returned. Online, shop only on secure connections and from sellers you or your family trust. Create a shopping email address you can filter and avoid posting your card's last four digits on social media, even as a joke. Tiny bits of public data make scammers' jobs easier.

Subscriptions and in-app purchases deserve special attention because they turn small taps into long drains. If a service is truly valuable, put its monthly cost into your budget and set a reminder to review it every quarter. If a game uses gems, coins, or skins that cost real money, tie purchases to family approval settings and keep the store password with an adult. If you want to test a subscription, add an end date on your calendar before the free trial begins. If you forget, the trial will remember you. Your goal is not to avoid every subscription; it is to keep only those that earn their place.

Travel and shared devices require upgrades to your routine. When you go on a trip, bring a backup way to pay and a paper list of emergency phone numbers for your bank and caregivers. If you must use a public computer to check a balance, sign out completely and change your password later on your own device. Never save card details in a browser you do not control. If a friend asks to "just use your card for a second," say no. Offer to help them find a safer option, but keep your accounts in your own hands. Kindness includes reasonable boundaries.

Case 1 — The Lost Card at the Arcade: You reach for your card and it is gone. Panic wants you to run in circles; your plan wants you to act. Step one: freeze the card in the bank app immediately so no new charges go through. Step two: check the app for recent transactions. If you see purchases you did not make, report them within the app or call the bank; ask a trusted adult to join the call. Step three: retrace your steps while the card is frozen. If you find it, unfreeze and carry on. If not, request a replacement. Because you froze fast, you turned a disaster into an annoyance.

Case 2 — The Surprise In-App Bill: Your sibling used your phone and approved several purchases in a game. You feel angry, then worried. Take screenshots of the charges, contact the app store through official support, and explain that a minor made unauthorized purchases. Many stores allow refunds for a first-time mistake. After the refund process, change your phone settings: require a password for every purchase, disable one-tap buys, and remove saved cards from the game. Then have a calm conversation at home about digital money rules. The problem was real; so is the fix.

Case 3 — The Shared Ride Mix-Up: A friend offers to call a ride for the group on their account if you send them your share. Later you discover their card failed and the driver charged a higher backup rate. Because you paid your friend in cash, you cannot dispute the charge. Next time, agree on the plan in advance: one person orders and shares the receipt, everyone pays through a traceable method, and an adult approves the route and pickup point. Convenience without clarity is a recipe for confusion.

Security does not end with lost cards and surprise bills. Learn to read your transaction list weekly. Look for tiny test charges from unknown companies—often a sign that someone is probing your account. If you see one, freeze the card and call right away. Enable two-factor authentication on your bank login so a thief needs more than a password to break in. Delete old cards from online shopping sites you no longer use. If a merchant you trust is breached, your bank can issue a new card; act fast, and keep your cool.

Privacy is part of protection. Many stores offer small discounts if you share big chunks of personal data. Ask yourself whether the discount is worth the inbox clutter and the tracking. Often the answer is no. If you do sign up, use that separate shopping email and uncheck boxes that allow sharing your information with "partners." Your money life should be quiet on purpose.

Payment apps that move money between friends can be useful, but they are not toys. Double-check the recipient before you hit send; money sent to a stranger is usually gone. Keep transactions private in the app settings; you are not writing a public diary of your snacks. When possible, tie the app to your debit card, not to an overdraft-enabled account. If the app offers buyer protection, read the rules before relying on it. These tools are best used with people you already know in real life.

Autopay can be a friend if you stay in charge. For bills you must pay on time, autopay prevents late fees. For wants and subscriptions, it can turn into sleep-paying for things you no longer use. Keep a short list of everything on autopay with the amount and date. Review the list every month and cancel at least one thing you no longer value. Momentum builds in both directions. Build it on purpose.

Closing thoughts for this chapter: Cards and digital wallets are not "grown-up problems." They are everyday tools you can master with a few steady habits. Understand the tool, set smart limits, freeze fast when something goes wrong, and keep your boundaries kind but firm. When you stay in charge of the taps and swipes, they serve your plan instead of steering it.

## Chapter 10 — Compound Growth and Inflation: Time at Work

Compound growth is what happens when your money earns a little extra, and then that extra also earns a little more. It is growth climbing on top of growth—slow at first, then steadier, then surprisingly strong over long stretches. You can think of it like planting a row of small trees. In year one, the saplings are fragile. In year three, they begin to shade the ground. In year seven, they are a line of shelter that changes the whole field. Compounding is not a trick; it is time doing quiet work.

Start with a simple picture. Imagine you place five dollars into savings every week. After ten weeks you have fifty dollars plus a bit of interest. After fifty weeks you have two hundred fifty dollars plus more interest. The interest looks tiny at the beginning—almost invisible. But if you keep going, interest gets to work not just on your deposits but also on the earlier interest. That is the "compound" part. The key is consistency. Compounding loves routines more than it loves large, dramatic gestures.

Now meet inflation, compounding's noisy neighbor. Inflation is the rise in prices over time. It makes yesterday's dollar buy a little less today. If a bus ticket was $1.50 last year and is $1.65 this year, that fifteen cents is inflation at work. Inflation is not always the same from year to year, and different things rise at different speeds—concert tickets, sneakers, and snacks may move differently than textbooks and bus fares. The lesson for you is not to panic; it is to plan. Build goals with a small cushion because prices drift.

Case 1 — Two Savers, Two Start Dates: Aiden and Noor both want $600 for a summer program. Aiden starts saving $12 a week in September. Noor waits until January and tries $20 a week. By June, Aiden has saved for forty weeks and reached the goal calmly, with several months of small interest along the way. Noor has only twenty-four weeks and must cut deeply into fun money to catch up. Neither kid is bad at money; they faced different calendars. The earlier start made time an ally for Aiden. Noor learned a lesson she can use next year: begin when the idea begins, not when the date is near.

Case 2 — The Camp Fee Surprise: Last year the camp cost $180. This year the invoice says $195. That is inflation plus camp costs changing. Because you kept a sinking fund—ten dollars a month across the year—the extra fifteen dollars did not hurt. You had a small cushion. If you had not prepared, you would feel frustrated and might blame the camp. With a cushion, you accept that prices move and you remember to update your chart for next year.

Rules of thumb can make compounding feel less abstract. Some people use the "rule of 72," which says you can estimate how long it takes something to double by dividing seventy-two by a growth rate. If a savings rate were roughly three percent, seventy-two divided by three equals about twenty-four years. If you found a safe place paying six percent, seventy-two divided by six equals about twelve years. These are estimates, not promises. Real life rarely grows in a straight line. The point is not the exact number; it is the direction: higher growth rates and longer time both make money stretch.

Compounding is not just for banks. Skills compound too. If you practice a musical instrument for fifteen minutes a day, your brain builds pathways that make tomorrow's fifteen minutes more effective. If you read thoughtfully every night, vocabulary stacks on vocabulary. When you learn to cook, the first pancake might burn; the tenth will not. Money and life share this truth: small, repeated actions beat rare bursts of effort.

Understanding inflation changes how you choose storage for money. Short-term money can sit safely in accounts that move easily. Long-term money—money for a goal far in the future—should live where it has a chance to grow enough to keep up with rising prices. The options vary by country and change over time. As a teen, your safest move is to learn the categories and ask adults to explain which are meant for short-term and which for long-term. The big mistake is using a short-term tool for a long-term job or vice versa.

Case 3 — Lump Sum vs. Weekly Habit: Jay receives $200 from a prize. Mia saves $5 a week from chores. Six months later, Jay still has most of the $200, but there is a dent from snacks and a gadget. Mia has roughly $120 saved with a clean chart and a strong habit. Who is "winning"? Both have money, but Mia has something Jay does not: a system that will keep working after the prize is gone. If Jay turns his prize into a weekly deposit—say, $5 of it every week—he can keep the feeling of momentum and avoid the slow leak of "just a little here, just a little there."

Patience is compounding's favorite friend. The first months feel boring. The numbers look small. You may be tempted to give up. That is why charts on a wall help: they make invisible growth visible. Color a square for every deposit; mark tiny interest payments on the side. When you see twenty colored squares, you will not want to break the chain. When you reach a milestone, take a photo of the chart and send it to the adult who cheered you on. Motivation grows when it is noticed.

Finally, guard against "too good to be true." Offers that promise to double your money quickly with no risk are not compounding; they are bait. Real growth is steady, not magical. Start safe. Ask questions until you understand. Let time do the heavy lifting. One day you will look back at that quiet chart and realize you built something strong with patience and simple math.

# Chapter 11 — Giving with Impact

Giving is not about guilt or perfection; it is about matching your care to real needs. When you give your time, attention, or money well, you change someone's day—and you change your own habits in ways that last. Start by choosing one or two causes that matter to you: animals at a local shelter, literacy at your library, trees in your neighborhood, a community pantry, or scholarships for younger players on your team. Write down exactly what you can offer this season: a percentage of your earnings, a fixed monthly amount, or a number of hours on specific weekends. Small, steady gifts punch far above their weight because organizations can count on them.

Do a little homework before you give money. Read the group's mission in their own words. Look for recent updates that show real activity. Ask a trusted adult to help you check whether the group is registered or recommended by reliable local sources. If you donate online, use the organization's official website, not a link from a comment, and keep the receipt. If you give through a collection box, note the exact name and address on the label so you can learn more later. Transparency is a form of respect in both directions.

Case 1 — The Library Wish List: Your town library posts a list of children's books and STEM kits they hope to buy. Instead of guessing what helps, you and two friends choose one item from the list, run a weekend lemonade stand with adult supervision, and donate the proceeds directly to that item. The librarian later shows you the kit in use. You feel the difference between vague giving and targeted giving. You also learn to ask groups what they actually need before you show up with bags of stuff they cannot use.

Volunteering is giving too. Many groups value people who can show up on time, listen to instructions, and finish tasks fully: sorting donations by size and season, packing food boxes to precise weights, reading with younger kids, cleaning up a park, or translating a flyer into another language you speak. Humility is the secret skill. Ask what would be most helpful rather than assuming you know. Replace yourself well by writing a one-page "how to" so the next volunteer can keep the work going smoothly.

Case 2 — The Team Equity Fund: Your recreation league quietly notices that talented players sometimes quit because gear and tournament fees are heavy. You propose a micro-fund inside the team, with coaches' approval, that families can donate to and that the coaches can use to cover costs anonymously for players who need help. You set clear rules and a short application that respects privacy.

Now the team keeps more players on the field, and your gift becomes an invisible net that catches kids before they fall out.

Fundraising needs the same honesty you expect from others. If you run a bake sale, label ingredients clearly. If you accept digital payments, use a name that identifies the cause and save receipts. Tell donors exactly what percentage goes to supplies and what percentage goes to the cause. If there is leftover cash after buying what you promised, report it and ask the group where it should go. Integrity is the heart of impact.

Impact also means checking that your help actually helped. Ask organizations how they measure success: number of meals delivered, books checked out, trees planted, hours coached. Look for outcomes, not only overhead numbers. A group with a perfect ratio but little activity is not as helpful as a small, steady team that consistently delivers. If your goal is to learn, request to shadow a staff member for an afternoon or to sit in on a planning meeting. Decision rooms teach lessons that public events cannot.

Case 3 — The Pantry Drive That Worked: Last year your class ran a food drive and delivered a mountain of random cans. This year you contact the pantry first. They ask for three specific items and for packages small enough for single households. You set a clear list, share it with families, and deliver exactly what was requested, sorted and labeled. The staff smiles because you saved them hours. You learn that listening multiplies generosity.

Keep giving joyful and sustainable. Do not promise more than you can do, and do not give to impress friends. Give because it matches your values and builds a world you want to live in. When money is tight, give time and attention. When time is tight, give money. When both are tight, give encouragement. A note that says "I see what you do and I'm grateful" is a real gift. Over time, you will discover that giving is not subtraction. It is addition by another name.

## Chapter 12 — Smart Shopping Online & Offline

Smart shopping starts long before you reach a store or open a browser. The simplest rule is two words: plan first. Write the item, the job it will do in your life, the features that matter, and the maximum you will spend. Decide in advance what counts as success: durability for a backpack, fit and ankle support for cleats, battery life for headphones. With a plan in your pocket, ads and aisle displays lose much of their power because you are busy comparing reality to your checklist, not sensations to wishes.

In a physical store, use your senses. Check seams, zippers, and stitching. Roll a suitcase down an aisle to feel the wheels. Put on a jacket and lift your arms. Read tags for materials and care. Ask a salesperson direct questions about return policies and warranties, and listen for specifics rather than vague promises. If a store offers a price match and you have solid proof, ask politely. If not, thank them and make your decision without drama. Polite firmness is a shopping superpower.

Online, become a detective. Read a mix of reviews, especially the middle-rated ones that explain both strengths and flaws. Check the seller's identity: are you buying from the brand itself or from a marketplace shop with a short history? Scan return windows and who pays for shipping. Beware of dark patterns—pages that hide the "no thanks" link, pre-check extra boxes, or shrink package sizes so the advertised price looks low. Keep a short list of trusted retailers your family uses; safety is worth a few dollars.

Case 1 — The Cleats Decision: Two pairs look similar. Pair A costs less but has thin stitching and weak ankle support. Pair B costs more, fits snugly, and comes with a six-month outsole warranty. You estimate hours of use and the cost per season. Pair B wins because it keeps your ankles safer and lasts the season without a mid-year replacement. You learn that the cheapest tag can be the most expensive choice if it fails early.

Case 2 — The Backpack Return: You bought a bag online that looked perfect. When it arrived, the straps dug into your shoulders and the zipper felt rough. Because you read the return policy before buying, you saved the packaging and requested a return within the window. The company sent a label and refunded your money. You spent ten minutes repacking and learned a durable skill: returns are part of smart shopping, not a hassle to fear.

Privacy is part of shopping, too. Many sites ask for more data than they need to fulfill an order. Give the minimum: shipping address, payment method, and an email for the receipt. Use strong passwords and a separate shopping email if you prefer. Unsubscribe from marketing emails that pull you into unplanned browsing. If a site offers a small discount in exchange for tracking your behavior across the web, weigh the cost in attention and privacy. Often the best savings is to close the tab and do something free.

Use price to tell time, not to tell worth. Holiday sales exist to move inventory, not to complete your identity. If your plan says "buy in March," and a February sale appears, check math, not mood. If it truly fits, great. If not, the deal is not a deal for you. Your calendar should be stronger than someone else's countdown clock.

Finally, respect the power of walking away. If a salesperson presses too hard, if the return policy feels slippery, or if the product's story does not match your need, say thank you and leave the cart empty. You just saved one hundred percent by not buying the wrong thing. Shopping is not a test of willpower; it is the practice of matching real needs to real solutions with calm and care.

## Chapter 13 — Scam & Fraud Safety

Scams succeed by rushing you, flattering you, or scaring you. Slow down, and you beat half of them in one move. A scammer may pretend to be a friend who lost a phone, a store offering a prize you never entered to win, a buyer who "overpays" and asks you to send back the difference, or a fake official who demands gift cards to fix a problem. The shapes change; the pressure feels the same. When someone insists on secrecy or speed, that demand is the alarm bell.

Learn the golden rules. Do not share one-time codes. Do not pay debts with gift cards. Do not click links in messages you did not expect. Do not send personal details or photos to strangers. If a message looks like it came from a company you use, go to the company's official app or website yourself, not through the link. Verify requests with a trusted adult before you act. Your goal is not to become a detective for every message; it is to build a simple habit: pause, verify, proceed.

Case 1 — The Fake Prize: You receive a text claiming you won a new console. All you need to do is click a link and enter a card to "confirm identity." You stop and show the text to your parent. Together you notice spelling errors, a weird web address, and a sense of hurry. You delete the message and block the number. That tiny pause saved you from a mess and taught you how false urgency feels in your body.

Online marketplaces need special care. Scammers list hot items at unbelievable prices, accept payment, and vanish. Others "overpay" with a fake check and ask you to refund the difference before the check bounces. Protect yourself by using cash or trusted digital methods with buyer/seller protection, meeting in safe, public locations with an adult, and refusing to ship until payment clears. If a buyer asks to move to a different platform or to send a code to "prove you are real," walk away. Real buyers and sellers respect reasonable rules.

Case 2 — The Imitation Friend: A DM arrives from a classmate's account asking for your phone number and a code "so I can add you to the group." You feel a twinge of doubt and ask the classmate in person the next day. They say their account was hacked. You report the DM as a scam. You also learn to keep group chats closed to invites from the inside, not from random links outside.

Keep devices and accounts locked. Use unique passwords, add two-factor authentication, and set alerts for logins from new locations. Review bank and wallet transactions weekly; small test charges are often the first sign that someone is probing your account. If you suspect fraud, report it immediately to your bank, the platform, and a trusted adult. Quicker reports lead to better outcomes. Being scammed is not a shame issue—it is a crime issue. What matters is responding fast and learning how the trick worked so you can spot its cousins later.

Case 3 — The Overpayment Trap: You sell a used bike online. A buyer claims they can only pay with a check and "accidentally" sends one for $200 more than the price, asking you to refund the difference immediately. Your bank shows the deposit as "pending," but the buyer pushes you to send the refund now. You decline, wait for the check to fully clear, and when it bounces you report the account. You keep your bike. You also keep your confidence.

Finally, remember that your calm is part of your security. Scammers try to move you off balance. Breathe, step back, and talk to someone you trust. Fear and flattery fade under daylight. Most of the time, the safest word in money is "no."

## Chapter 14 — The Psychology of Money

Money is not only math; it is mood, memory, and meaning. Your brain uses shortcuts to save time, and some of those shortcuts bend your money without asking permission. Present bias makes now feel heavier than later, so a quick treat wins over a distant goal. Social proof makes you want what your group wants, even if their needs differ from yours. The sunk-cost fallacy urges you to keep paying for a subscription you do not use because you "already paid." Anchoring lets the first price you see pull your judgment toward it, even when it is unrelated. None of this means you are weak. It means you are human.

Design your environment so the smart choice is the easy choice. Put friction in front of habits you want less of: remove stored cards from shopping sites, uninstall one tap-to-buy app, and add a twenty-four-hour pause rule for non-essential purchases. Remove friction from habits you want more of: set automatic transfers to savings on allowance day, keep a water bottle by the door, and put your library card next to your computer. A two-minute setup can change dozens of future decisions.

Case 1 — The Sleepover Snack Spiral: Every Friday after practice, your group hits the convenience store and you spend without thinking. You run an experiment. You bring a snack from home, keep $2 cash in your pocket for something small, and put your card away. After three Fridays, you realize you had the same fun for a third of the cost. You did not need perfect willpower; you needed a tiny plan that met the real need—time with friends and a treat—without opening your wallet wide.

Reframe stories that no longer serve you. "I'm bad at saving" becomes "I'm learning to save by moving $5 first." "I can't say no to friends" becomes "I say yes to friends and no to pressure." "I'm not a money person" becomes "I'm building money skills the same way I built my jump shot—practice and review." Language is a lever. Use it to lift yourself instead of pinning yourself down.

Case 2 — The Decoy Price: A streaming service shows three plans. The middle one is highlighted as "Best Value," the highest one is overpriced on purpose to make the middle seem cheap, and the lowest one looks weak. You pause, list what you actually need, and pick the lowest plan with a reminder to review in a month. Anchoring loses power because you anchored to your needs, not to their design.

Gratitude and goals are a powerful pair. Gratitude shrinks the feeling that you are missing out by naming what is already good: a library full of books, a team that accepts you, a safe home, a working phone. Goals give your brain something exciting to chase. Before you browse stores, name three free or already-paid joys. After you plan a purchase, write the reason on a card. When gratitude goes first and goals follow, ads do not stand a chance.

Case 3 — The Sunk-Cost Subscription: You signed up for a study app during exam season and forgot to cancel. Months later you feel guilty and keep paying because "I've already spent so much." You cancel anyway, write a one-line rule—"subscriptions need a start date and a review date"—and set a calendar check in three months. You saved future money and freed yourself from a mental knot. Sunk-cost feelings are loud; future freedom is louder.

Finally, be kind to yourself as you build money skills. No one avoids every bias or every impulsive buy. We learn by making small mistakes while the numbers are small. The win is not being perfect. The win is catching yourself one decision earlier than last time and designing your world so the next right step is easy and obvious.

# Chapter 15 — Negotiation Basics for Teens

Negotiation is respectful problem-solving where both sides try to meet important needs. You already negotiate daily—who gets the last seat, which movie to watch, how late a game can run. Money negotiations include allowances and chores, the price of a used bike, or the fee for a small job. The goal is not to "win"; the goal is to work together so value increases for both sides.

Preparation is your advantage. Know what you want, why it matters, what you can trade, and your best alternative if you cannot agree. In grown-up terms this is your BATNA—Best Alternative To a Negotiated Agreement. If you are offering lawn care, your BATNA might be finding a different client next door or spending the time on another paying task. If you are asking for a raise in your allowance, your BATNA might be proposing extra responsibilities that justify the change.

Open with a calm, clear ask. Use numbers and reasons: "I can mow your lawn every Saturday this month. That's four visits. Would $40 for the month work, paid each Saturday so we both stay on schedule?" Then be quiet and let the other person think. Silence is a tool, not a threat. If they counter, listen for what really matters to them—reliability, speed, quality—and offer solutions that serve those needs. You might adjust scope instead of price: "If I also sweep the steps, would $12 per visit be fair?"

Case 1 — The Bike Price: You find a used bike for $120. You research similar models and see they sell for $90–$130 depending on condition. In person, you point out a worn tire and a squeaky brake and offer $100, cash, today. The seller counters at $110. You accept with one request: that they include the small tool kit pictured in the ad. You leave with a fair deal and a lesson—specific reasons plus respectful tone beat arguing.

Write down agreements so memories do not fight later. A short message that lists the job, the price, the time, the place, and what happens if plans change is enough. Send it before you begin. When the work is done, send a thank-you and ask for a short note you can use as a reference. References compound future opportunities.

Case 2 — The Allowance Conversation: You ask caregivers to adjust your allowance because your responsibilities have grown. You prepare a one-page list of current tasks, the time they take, and three new tasks you are ready to add. You propose a number and an evaluation date one month later. They may say yes, no, or "let's try a smaller increase with the new tasks." You accept a trial and set the date on the calendar. Because you prepared, the talk stays calm and focused on value, not volume.

Know when to walk away. If someone is rude, if the terms keep changing, or if a job feels unsafe, end the conversation politely. Your reputation is more valuable than any single deal. Likewise, know when to say yes. A slightly lower price with a reliable client may be worth more than a high price with a headache. Think like a long-term partner, not a one-time winner.

Finally, practice at safe tables. Negotiate chores and privileges at home; negotiate deadlines and roles on team projects at school. Pay attention to what worked: asking clear questions, summarizing agreements out loud, and proposing options that solve the other side's problem. Negotiation is a muscle; it grows with use.

## Chapter 16 — Planning Big Goals

Big goals—like a bike, a class trip, an instrument upgrade, or specialized lessons—feel heavy until you turn them into steps. Begin with one sentence that names the number, the date, and the reason: "I will save $300 by March 31 for a keyboard so I can practice with the school jazz band." Put the sentence where you will see it daily. Goals are more likely to happen when they are visible and meaningful.

Break the number into chunks you can actually reach. If March 31 is twelve weeks away, $300 becomes $25 per week. List the real costs: not only the price tag, but the accessories, the case, batteries, lessons, transport, and time. Look for ways to shrink costs without shrinking joy: borrow gear to test before buying, buy used from trusted sources, trade skills with a friend, or share rides to cut travel expenses.

Create a sinking fund—a special container for this goal only. Pay it first the moment money arrives so you do not use leftovers. Track progress on a chart you can color or check off. Progress you can see keeps motivation alive. Ask for allies: a family member who matches part of what you save, a friend who wants the same goal so you can encourage each other, a teacher who points you to scholarships or discounts. Invite accountability gently, not as pressure but as support.

Case 1 — The Trip Budget: Your class trip to the science center is two months away. Ticket: $18. Bus: $7. Lunch: you can pack or buy. You price both and choose to pack, saving $6. You set a plan: $5 a week into the trip fund, plus one small side job to cover the last bit. You add a back-up plan: if the side job falls through, you will pause your streaming subscription for one month. The plan feels calm because you handled the details.

Expect turbulence. A birthday invitation appears, prices change, or a ride falls through. When the plan wobbles, adjust steps, not the dream. Extend the date, add a tiny job, sell two items you no longer use, or pause a low-value expense. If you fall behind completely, rewrite the one-line goal and begin again. Goals are not all-or-nothing; they are maps you redraw as you learn the landscape.

Case 2 — The Instrument Upgrade: You want to upgrade from a starter violin to an intermediate one. New, it costs too much. With your teacher's help, you try several used violins and find one in excellent condition for half the price, including a case and bow. You agree on a return window so you can get a second opinion. You clean and maintain the instrument carefully. The upgrade feels like a victory not just because of the sound, but because the plan respected your budget and your timeline.

Build momentum with milestone moments. Every time you cross ten percent, do something small that supports the goal—watch a tutorial, organize your practice space, or write a thank-you to your future self. Do not celebrate by undoing progress. Matching rewards to the journey keeps your brain excited without draining your fund.

Finally, link goals to identity. If you see yourself as someone who keeps promises—including money promises to your future self—choices simplify. The snack you skip is not a loss; it is a vote for the musician, traveler, or athlete you are becoming. The chart you color is not childish; it is discipline in friendly ink. Big goals become possible when you design your environment so the next right step is easy to take.

## Chapter 17 — Start a Mini Venture

A mini venture is a tiny, safe business that solves a simple problem for people you can reach. Begin with service: what can you do that helps? Pet sitting with adult supervision, organizing digital photos for grandparents, teaching a beginner skill you know well, selling pre-ordered baked goods at a family event, or repairing loose bike chains for neighbors. Keep it small enough to learn without big risk.

Sketch a one-page plan that names your customer, the problem, your solution, your price, your costs, and how you will deliver. Keep it simple: "Busy families need reliable pet care during weekends. I will feed, water, and play with cats and send a photo update for $10 per day under adult supervision." Safety and permission come first—follow family rules and local guidelines, especially for food and home visits.

Test before you invest. Ask three potential customers whether your idea would help and what they would pay. Start with pre-orders so you do not buy materials you cannot sell. If you bake, calculate ingredients, labels, and packaging; set a price that covers costs plus a fair profit. If you teach, plan the lesson and gather materials. Deliver on time and a little better than promised.

Case 1 — The Pre-Order Cookie Sale: You post a menu with two flavors for pickup on Saturday, limit orders to what you can bake safely in one evening with a parent present, and close orders on Thursday. You collect payments in advance and schedule pickup windows. On Saturday you deliver neat boxes with labels and thank-you notes. Costs and profits are clear because you sold before you baked.

Keep records of every cost and every payment; profit is what remains after costs, not just the money you collected. Set aside a small percentage of profit to reinvest in better tools or training. Ask for short testimonials and permission to use first names. Share results with your family; they are your advisors.

Case 2 — The Bike-Fix Pop-Up: On a sunny weekend you set up a small stand with a sign: "Free chain checks; $5 to adjust brakes; $3 to inflate and check tires." You work on the sidewalk in front of your home with adult supervision. You bring basic tools, a clean cloth, and a smile. You keep a simple queue and accept small digital payments. At day's end you have earned modestly and learned enormously—how to greet, how to explain, and how to pace yourself.

Close the loop with reflection. What went well? What was hard? What will you change next time? Improve one piece per round: a clearer sign, a better booking form, or a more accurate estimate. End the venture when the season ends or your schedule changes; success includes knowing when to stop. The point is not to become a mogul—it is to practice creating value and getting paid in a safe, supervised way.

Finally, remember that ventures grow from trust. Be honest when you are booked, communicate changes early, and keep promises. Your first customers are neighbors and family friends; treat them like long-term partners. Reliability is rare and therefore valuable. If you earn a reputation for showing up, you will never lack for opportunities.

## Chapter 18 — Taxes & Teen Work (Basics)

Taxes fund things communities share—roads, schools, libraries, parks, and services that keep people safe. Rules differ by country and even by city, and they change as governments update them. What teens need is a high-level map and good record-keeping habits. If you work for an employer, your pay stub may show that money was withheld for taxes or social programs before you receive it. Keep every pay slip and read it so you understand what happened to your gross pay and what you actually took home.

Case 1 — Reading a Pay Stub: You work twelve hours at a snack stand for $12 per hour. You expect $144 but receive $129.60. The pay stub shows that a portion went to taxes and a social insurance program. With a guardian, you learn which parts are standard where you live and whether any forms are needed at year's end. You also learn to plan for "take-home pay," the amount after withholdings, not just the headline number.

If you earn money directly from customers—selling crafts, tutoring, mowing lawns—keep a simple ledger. Record the date, the amount received, and any costs like materials or transport. Save receipts and screenshots. In some places you may owe taxes on profits at the end of the year; in others, small amounts below a threshold may not require filing. Because the rules vary, ask a trusted adult or teacher to help you find official guidance for students in your area. Do not guess; guesswork leads to stress.

Case 2 — The Craft Table: You sell handmade bracelets at a family event. You earn $180 and spend $65 on beads and cord. Your profit is $115. You record the numbers, save a few photos, and put a portion aside in case taxes apply where you live. You learn that revenue is not the same as profit and that tidy records turn tax season from panic into paperwork.

Some teens also receive small interest from savings accounts. Keep those statements; they may be part of your record even if no action is required this year. If you donate money to registered charities, keep those receipts too. They may matter for your family's filing, depending on local rules.

Never ignore letters from tax authorities; show them to an adult promptly. Scams also pretend to be tax messages. Real agencies do not demand gift cards or threaten arrest over text. If a message scares you, pause and verify through official channels. Honesty is cheaper than penalties, and learning the basics early saves you stress later.

Finally, remember you do not need to know every detail right now. You need to know where to look, who to ask, and how to keep clean records. Taxes are a shared responsibility, and the grown-ups around you are part of your team. Ask questions, learn steadily, and you will be ready as your work grows.

## Chapter 19 — Debt & Borrowing Basics

Debt is borrowing money you promise to pay back later, usually with extra cost called interest. Adults use debt for homes, education, or businesses; debt can also trap people who borrow for things that do not last. For teens, the main lessons are caution and clarity. Borrow only with adult guidance, borrow for needs not whims, and know the total you will repay, not just the monthly piece. A low monthly payment with a very long timeline can cost far more than it seems.

Case 1 — The Phone Plan Illusion: A shiny new phone "only $25 a month!" sounds affordable until you read the fine print—thirty-six months at that price, plus fees. The total is $900 before taxes and insurance. If your current phone works, saving toward a used or discounted model might be smarter. If you must finance, compare total cost across the full term and choose the shortest timeline you can truly afford.

Credit cards deserve special care. They are tools adults use to pay now and settle the bill later; if the balance is not paid in full each month, interest can pile up fast. Minimum payments look friendly but extend debt for years. Small, high-cost loans from untrustworthy lenders grow into large problems quickly. If you must borrow, compare offers by the annual percentage rate (APR) and all fees, read every line of the agreement, and ask an adult to review it with you.

Borrowing between friends and family is emotional. If you lend, only lend what you can afford not to see again, and write down the terms kindly—amount, date, and plan for repayment. If you borrow, propose a clear schedule and keep it. Missed promises damage trust more than they damage wallets. Often the best answer is to avoid borrowing altogether by saving ahead or adjusting the plan.

Case 2 — The Club Trip: Your team announces a surprise tournament. You are short $60. Instead of borrowing, you ask the coach for ways to earn it: setting up equipment, helping with younger teams, or selling a small batch of team stickers with permission. You reach the amount in a week and arrive at the tournament proud. You bought not only the trip but also your independence.

Finally, learn the positive alternative to debt: patience. A tiny delay can save you from heavy costs. If you must borrow later for adult goals, you will do it with eyes open—understanding the math, the timeline, and the trade-offs. That confidence starts now with simple, debt-free wins.

## Chapter 20 — Family Money Talks & Values

Families shape how you feel about money long before you handle it yourself. Create a gentle habit of talking about choices, not secrets. Ask caregivers how they decide between brands, how they compare unit prices, and how they plan for big expenses. If your family uses an allowance or pays for chores, write the rules together: what counts as a family responsibility and what counts as extra work, what the pay is, when it arrives, and what happens if the job is late. Clarity prevents arguments and teaches responsibility.

Hold simple family money meetings—fifteen minutes, once a month. Celebrate wins, review goals, and choose one small improvement for the month ahead. Post a shared calendar for upcoming costs like birthdays and trips so surprises are rarer. Encourage siblings to respect each other's savings goals and to ask before borrowing items. When mistakes happen—and they will—focus on fixing the system rather than blaming the person. Values make rules sustainable.

Case 1 — The Grocery Challenge: One Saturday you and a caregiver plan a week of dinners. You set a budget, make a list, and shop together, comparing unit prices and store brands. At home you calculate savings and add part of it to a family fun jar. You learn that planning turns money into meals and that teamwork reduces stress for everyone.

Case 2 — The Allowance Reset: Arguments keep popping up about what the allowance covers. You propose a reset. Together you list which items are family-paid (school supplies, basic clothes) and which are teen-paid (extra treats, brand upgrades). You set paydays and add a rule: "If the job is late, the pay is late." Disagreements shrink because the map got clearer.

Talk about giving and community, too. Decide as a family which causes to support this season and how to split the gift between money and volunteering. Share stories about a time someone helped your family and a time you helped someone else. Money becomes less stressful when it is connected to purpose.

Finally, remember that family money talks are about growth, not grades. No one gets everything right. If a plan fails, update it. If a purchase disappoints, learn why. If someone feels left out, adjust. When you treat money as a shared project, you build trust and skills that last far beyond any single bill or budget.

# Chapter 21 — Money Tools That Work: Spreadsheets, Envelopes, and Apps

Tools do not replace habits; they support them. The best money tool is the one you will actually use with calm regularity. For many teens, three options cover almost every need: a simple spreadsheet, a physical or digital envelope system, and a lightweight budgeting app with clear categories. Each one has strengths. Spreadsheets show the math and let you customize. Envelopes force real choices by separating money for different jobs. Apps keep your plan in your pocket and send alerts before your plan drifts.

Start with the spreadsheet because it teaches first principles. Create four columns labeled date, description, category, and amount. Add two simple tables: expected income and planned expenses. When money arrives, enter it. When money leaves, enter it. At week's end, sort by category and total the columns. You will see reality faster than you think. Spreadsheets are honest mirrors. If you love them, you can add gentle formulas that total categories automatically and highlight when you exceed your plan. If you dislike them, use them for one month only to build awareness, then shift to envelopes or an app.

Envelopes, whether paper or digital, make priorities visible. Label one envelope for saving, one for sharing, and several for spending categories you choose: transport, snacks, hobbies, gifts, school. When money arrives, fill the envelopes according to your plan. If the snack envelope empties on Wednesday, your choice is not to raid another envelope; your choice is to wait. Waiting is not punishment; it is how you protect the promises you made to your future self. Digital envelopes in a banking app or a budgeting app behave similarly, but paper envelopes teach the feeling of limits in a way screens cannot.

Apps bring convenience if you stay in charge. Choose one that allows manual entry and simple categories rather than chasing complex features that you will not use. Turn on alerts for low balances and upcoming bills. If the app connects to your bank, review the category rules it guesses and fix them when they are wrong. An app is a helpful assistant, not a brain replacement. If it confuses you, try a simpler one or return to envelopes and a calendar.

Cases show how tools fit different lives. In the first case, a student with irregular weekend earnings uses envelopes. They split each cash burst into predetermined portions, keep envelopes in a safe place, and stop spending when a category is empty. Their stress falls because they no longer guess how much remains. In the second case, a student who loves computers uses a spreadsheet to track every purchase for four weeks. They discover that small streaming charges added up to more than basketball fees. They cancel two subscriptions and move the savings to a sinking fund for new shoes. In the third case, a busy athlete uses a minimal app only for three tasks: setting a weekly snack budget, logging bus fares, and getting a reminder the night before a monthly club due. The app's strength is not charts; it is timing.

Calendars and reminders are part of your tool kit. Put recurring costs on the dates they happen. Set a tiny alarm every Friday to do a ten minute review. Link your reminders to routines you already keep.

If you review right after last class on Friday, your brain will soon expect the rhythm. If you prefer Sunday, pair it with a drink and a chair you like and keep the session short and friendly.

Security is also a tool. Protect files with a device password and back them up. Use strong, unique passwords for any app that touches money. Do not share screenshots of your balances; privacy is safety. Talk with a trusted adult about which features to use and which to avoid. A helpful rule is to keep any automation reversible. If a transfer happens automatically, you should be able to stop it just as easily if life changes.

Finally, choose one tool to start and commit for thirty days. At the end, ask three questions. Did this tool show me reality? Did it help me act sooner? Did I feel calmer using it? If the answers are mostly yes, keep going. If not, switch. The right tool for your friend may not be the right tool for you. Your goal is not to be trendy; it is to be steady.

# Chapter 22 — Read Statements and Receipts: Bank, Card, and Wallet Literacy

Financial literacy means being able to read the paperwork your money leaves behind. A statement tells the story of a month. A receipt tells the story of a purchase. Together they help you spot errors, stay on budget, and understand where your effort went. This chapter teaches you to read these documents calmly, without fear.

Begin with bank statements. The top line lists the account name, the period it covers, and the starting and ending balances. Below that you see deposits, withdrawals, and fees in date order. Check whether the beginning balance of this month matches the ending balance of last month. Scan deposits to make sure your allowance or pay landed. Review withdrawals for purchases and transfers you recognize. If you see a fee, read the description and ask the bank how to avoid it next time. Statements are teachers that never raise their voice; they simply show what happened.

Card statements add a few wrinkles. Debit card statements list where you used your card and how much was deducted from your bank. Credit card statements, usually for adults, show a statement balance, a minimum payment, and a due date. Learn the vocabulary even if a caregiver handles the account. The minimum payment is the smallest amount the bank will accept to keep the account in good standing, but paying only the minimum creates expensive interest. The statement balance is the full amount you owe for that period. The due date is the date by which payment must arrive to avoid a late fee. Knowing these terms early makes you a calmer reader later.

Digital wallets show transaction histories inside apps. Tap to see the merchant, the time, the amount, and sometimes the location. Some apps show pending charges that have not finalized yet; they may adjust slightly when they settle. Learn to distinguish pending from posted. If a charge looks wrong, do not panic. First check whether it is a hold, such as a small test charge or a temporary amount for a ride. If it still looks wrong after a day, contact the merchant through official channels and your bank if needed.

Receipts are evidence and memory. When you buy something that may need to be returned or warrantied, keep the receipt in a safe place or scan it. A good receipt shows the date, the exact item, the price, any discount, sales tax if your region applies it, and the total paid. If you pay partly with cash and partly with a gift card, the receipt should show both. If the cashier types the wrong code or the discount does not apply, ask politely in the moment. Fixing errors later is harder than fixing them while you are standing at the counter.

Cases illustrate the value of careful reading. In one case, you notice a $1.00 charge from a company you do not recognize on your statement. Rather than ignoring it because it is small, you call your bank with a caregiver. It turns out to be a test charge from a compromised card number. Your bank issues a new card and blocks the old one. You saved yourself from future fraud by noticing a tiny clue. In another case, your bus app shows a double charge. You take screenshots, note the time, and submit a ticket through the app. The company refunds the duplicate ride. You learn that prompt, polite reports work.

Reconciliation is a big word for a simple habit: match your records to the bank's records. If you keep a spreadsheet or an app, compare your list of purchases to the statement once a month. Put a small check mark next to each item that matches. If something is missing from your list, add it. If something appears on your list but not on the statement, check whether it is pending. Reconciliation keeps surprises small. It also reduces the anxiety of not knowing. The numbers are your team, not your enemy.

Finally, adopt a quiet ritual for paperwork. At month's end, download or file your statements, save receipts associated with items you might return or warranty claims, and shred sensitive papers you no longer need. Knowing where documents live and how to read them lets you move through money life with confidence. You will make mistakes sometimes; everyone does. But with clear eyes, you will also catch them and learn.

# Chapter 23 — Insurance Basics for Teens: Protect People, Stuff, and Plans

Insurance looks boring until the day it looks brilliant. It is a tool that gathers many people's small payments to cover the big, rare problems that are too heavy for one person to carry alone. For teens, the goal is not to buy policies on your own; it is to understand the idea so you can participate in family decisions and protect your future when you are older.

Think of three categories: people, stuff, and plans. People includes health and sometimes life insurance that protects families against huge medical bills or the loss of a caregiver's income. Stuff includes coverage for things like a family car, bikes, or electronics under certain policies. Plans includes travel insurance for trips and event insurance for important occasions. Each policy defines what is covered, what is not, how much you pay regularly (the premium), and how much you must pay out of pocket when something happens (the deductible).

Health insurance, where available, helps families pay for doctor visits, prescriptions, and emergencies. It often comes with a network of approved providers and different costs for different services. For teens, the key habit is to carry your health card if your family uses one and to know how to reach a caregiver in an emergency. Do not sign forms you do not understand; ask an adult to explain. Keep receipts from clinics and pharmacies in case your family needs them for records.

Property coverage sometimes protects items you use, even if you do not own a policy yourself. For example, a family's homeowners or renters insurance may cover theft of a bike from a locked area or certain damage to personal items, subject to deductibles and limits. The details vary by policy and by place. Learn the rules where you live. Write down serial numbers for electronics, store photos of valuables, and lock your gear. Prevention is the cheapest form of insurance.

Travel insurance matters when you plan big trips. It can cover canceled flights, lost luggage, or medical issues away from home, depending on the policy. Teens traveling with school groups should know who holds the policy, what the emergency phone number is, and where the coverage documents live. If someone suggests skipping travel insurance to save a few dollars, consider the risk of losing the entire trip cost. A small premium is sometimes the price of sleeping well.

Cases show how insurance touches real life. In one case, your violin is damaged when a water pipe leaks at school. Your family's policy covers personal property damaged by sudden leaks, but the deductible is high. You and your caregiver decide whether making a claim is worth it or if paying for the repair yourselves is cheaper in the long run. You learn that insurance is not free money; it is a contract with trade-offs. In another case, your friend's phone is stolen at a café. The store's sign says "not responsible for lost items." They ask whether any policy covers it. You learn that some family policies include limited coverage for theft outside the home, but only with a police report and proof of purchase. You help your friend gather documents and learn to register new devices in the future.

Read policies with curiosity, not dread. Focus on the definitions section, the list of what is covered, the list of exclusions, the deductible, and the claim steps. Ask what evidence is required if something happens—photos, serial numbers, receipts, a report. Encourage your family to store important documents in two places: a physical folder and a secure digital folder with backups. When you know where to look, emergencies feel less chaotic.

Insurance is not a replacement for caution. Lock your bike, use a case for devices, avoid risky shortcuts, and keep emergency contacts handy. Insurance is the seatbelt, not the driver. It does not prevent bad things, but it reduces how much they hurt. Understanding it now prepares you for adult decisions later and helps your family today.

## Chapter 24 — Investing 101 (Education Only): Risk, Return, and Diversification

This chapter is education, not a recommendation to buy anything. Investing means putting money into something with the hope that it will grow over time, knowing that it can go up or down along the way. The purpose of learning about investing now is to understand the language and the ideas so that when you are older and the time is right, you can make informed choices with a trusted adult's guidance and according to the rules where you live.

Risk and return travel together. If an investment promises higher potential returns, it usually carries higher risk—meaning the price can drop in the short term, sometimes sharply. Lower-risk places, like insured savings accounts, grow slowly but protect your money from big swings. Knowing your time horizon matters. Money you will need soon belongs in safer places. Money for goals far in the future might handle more ups and downs because you have time to wait.

Diversification is a long word for a simple idea: do not put all your eggs in one basket. If you own a small piece of many different companies or bonds through a fund, one disappointing result will not sink your whole plan. Diversification does not remove risk; it spreads it so you do not depend on a single lucky guess. Many adults use broad index funds to diversify at low cost, but the availability and rules for teens vary by country. The principle applies everywhere: variety reduces the chance that one mistake hurts too much.

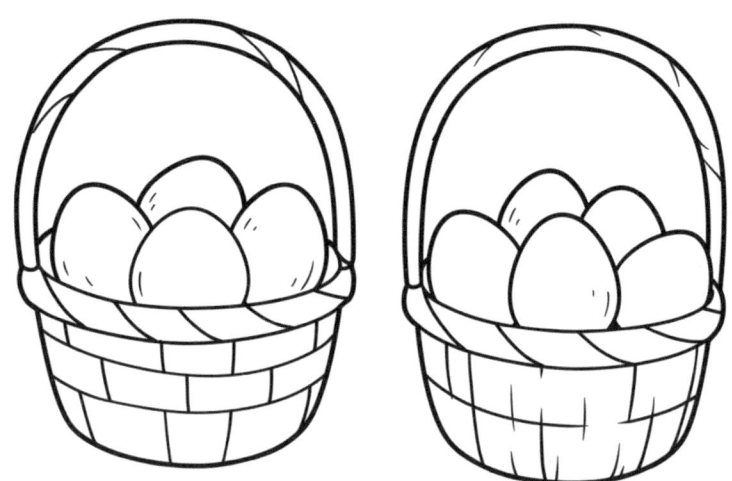

Volatility is the wiggle in the line. Prices move every day because people in markets change their minds about what things are worth. If you watch the wiggles too closely, you may feel seasick and make emotional decisions. Learning the history of markets teaches patience. Over long stretches, diversified investments have often grown more than cash, but they never move in a straight line and they do not come with guarantees.

Cases make the ideas concrete. In one case, you hear a classmate brag about a "hot stock" that doubled last month. You feel fear of missing out. You and a caregiver read an article about how single stocks can move wildly and how yesterday's jump does not predict tomorrow's result. You decide that, for now, your learning will happen with simulations and small practice accounts if they are allowed, not with money you cannot afford to lose. In another case, you compare two imaginary portfolios. One is a single trendy company. The other is a broad mix of many companies through a low-cost fund. You simulate a year of ups and downs. The fund's line wiggles but survives. The single stock soars, then suddenly falls. You learn why diversification exists.

Costs matter because they quietly eat returns. Fees for buying, selling, or managing money reduce what you keep. A small percentage taken year after year compounds in the wrong direction. Adults who invest often compare fees carefully. When you are older, you will ask the same questions: what is the total cost, how is it charged, and what do I get in return? Transparency is a sign of trustworthiness.

Behavior matters as much as math. Investors get in their own way by chasing what is hot, panicking at dips, or forgetting their plan. The cure is a written plan that says why you are investing, for how long, how you will diversify, and when you will review. As a teen, your "plan" is to study the vocabulary, practice with pretend portfolios if allowed, and develop the patience to let compounding do its work in the future.

Finally, remember that investing is optional for teens and should always happen with adult guidance and within local laws. Your primary wins now are building skills, earning safely, saving with purpose, and avoiding debt. If you master those four, you will be ready for investing lessons when the time comes.

## Chapter 25 — Use Money for Good: Philanthropy, Social Enterprise, and Everyday Ethics

Money is not only for private goals. It is also a way to shape the world around you. Philanthropy is organized giving to causes you care about. Social enterprise is a business that aims to solve a problem while earning enough to keep going. Everyday ethics is the way you choose what to buy and from whom. All three are within reach for teens when you start small and stay practical.

Begin with purpose. Write one sentence about what you want to support this season. It might say, "I will help younger readers build confidence," or "I will reduce waste at school," or "I will support the local park where my team practices." Purpose focuses your giving and your projects. With a parent or teacher, identify one organization to partner with or one specific change you can lead. Real impact comes from alignment and follow-through.

Philanthropy can be systematic even when amounts are small. Set a percentage of your income to give—perhaps five or ten percent—and move it to a separate envelope or digital bucket when money arrives. Once a month, donate to the partner you chose and write a short note about why you care. Ask how small gifts are used and how to volunteer. Keep receipts so you can see your impact accumulate over time. The habit matters as much as the amount.

Social enterprise starts with a problem you can help solve. If single-use bottles fill your school trash, you could sell low-cost reusable bottles with the school logo and donate a portion of profit to the green club. If kids at your park get sunburned at games, you could run a small stand with hats and sunscreen at cost, funded by sponsors who care about safety. Keep your projects safe, small, and transparent. Post your costs and your donations so trust grows.

Everyday ethics shows up each time you buy. You can choose durable items over disposables, repair instead of replace, buy used where appropriate, and support local makers when prices and quality align. You can avoid companies that treat people or the planet poorly when you have good information. Perfection is not the goal; awareness is. You will not always have the budget to buy the most ethical option. When you cannot, you can reduce waste and take good care of what you do buy.

Cases illustrate the range of action. In one case, you and two friends run a one-day park cleanup followed by a picnic. You plan, get permission, set a clear time limit, provide gloves and bags, and take a photo of the filled bins. You then write to the city asking for more recycling bins near the soccer fields. Your project is visible and complete. In another case, you launch a mini venture selling notebooks made from recycled paper. You price them fairly, donate a set to the school writing club, and publish a simple statement showing how many notebooks you sold and how many were given. You learn that trust grows when numbers are open.

Be careful with claims about "green" or "fair" products. Read labels and look for independent certifications where available. Do not shame friends or family for different choices; invite them to join you by making your actions easy to copy. Celebrate progress instead of policing perfection. Money for good is about building momentum.

Finally, reflect on how giving and ethical choices make you feel. Keep a short journal of what you tried, what worked, and what you would change. Share results with mentors who can connect you to bigger projects when you are ready. When money becomes a tool for kindness and repair, your life feels larger and your skills grow.

# Chapter 26 — Consumer Rights and Wise Returns: Warranties, Guarantees, and Fixing Problems

Consumers have rights, and companies have responsibilities. Knowing the basics helps you solve problems calmly and fairly. When you buy something that does not work as promised, you are not stuck with frustration. You have steps you can take.

Start at the beginning: read policies before you buy. A return policy explains if and how you can return an item, and within what time. A warranty is a promise that a product will work for a certain period; if it fails during that time under normal use, the company will repair, replace, or refund it according to the terms. Guarantees and "satisfaction promises" add another layer. Keep copies of these policies or bookmark the pages when you purchase. Store receipts in a safe place or scan them.

Approach returns and exchanges with politeness and facts. Bring the item, the receipt, the original packaging if possible, and a short description of the problem. Explain clearly what happened and what you are asking for—refund, exchange, repair, or store credit according to the policy. Do not exaggerate. Staff are more likely to help when you are calm and prepared. If a frontline worker cannot help, ask kindly for a supervisor. Most problems are solved at this level when you bring documentation.

Cases show how preparation pays. In one case, your headphones stop charging after three months. You check the warranty: one year for defects. You bring the receipt, the box, and the product to the store. The staff tests the charger and the port, confirms a fault, and exchanges the unit. You leave relieved because you kept your paperwork. In another case, you buy a jacket online and the zipper breaks the first week. The seller's site shows a thirty-day return window for defective items. You take photos, print the policy, and file the request. A replacement arrives without drama. You learn that returns are part of responsible shopping, not a fight.

Sometimes a company denies a reasonable request. Breathe and choose your next step. If the item was sold by a marketplace seller, contact the platform and provide evidence. If the charge was incorrect, dispute it through your bank or card within the allowed time. If the case involves safety, contact local consumer protection agencies. Always use official channels and keep your words professional. The goal is resolution, not revenge.

Warranties do not cover every problem. Damage from abuse or unauthorized repairs is usually excluded. Read carefully before you decide which path to take. Sometimes a local repair shop can fix a non-warranty issue for a fair price and save the object from the trash. Learning basic maintenance extends the life of your things and reduces how often you need to return anything at all.

Keep a small "problem-solving kit" at home: a folder for receipts and warranties, a notepad for dates and names, and a habit of photographing serial numbers. If you must ship an item, pack it well and use trackable methods. If a refund appears, it may take days to show on a card; note the expected timeline so you do not worry needlessly.

Finally, remember that rights come with responsibilities. Be honest about how the problem happened. Do not exploit policies to get free upgrades. Treat workers with respect. When you model fairness and firmness together, you often get better outcomes—and you build a reputation as someone companies want to help.

## Chapter 27 — Sustainable Spending: Repair, Reuse, and the Hidden Life of Things

Every dollar you spend touches the planet. Products have hidden lives: raw materials are gathered, factories shape them, trucks move them, stores display them, and finally you use and discard them. Sustainable spending means choosing items and habits that reduce waste, save money over time, and keep value in circulation. It is not about perfection. It is about better choices, one at a time.

Begin with durability. Buy items that last and that can be repaired. Look for replaceable parts, standard screws, and clear maintenance instructions. A backpack with strong stitching and a lifetime repair policy may cost more today and much less over three school years. A water bottle with a spare-parts page on the brand's site is a sign of respect for customers and for the planet. Durability protects your budget and reduces trash.

Repair is a superpower. Learn basic fixes—sewing a button, mending a small tear, patching a tube, cleaning a charging port, replacing a strap. Watch a few approved tutorials with an adult and practice on low-risk items. A small repair kit at home saves money and gives you pride. If a repair is beyond you, ask a local shop for a quote before you replace the item. Many towns have community "fix-it" events where volunteers teach repairs for free. The more you repair, the more you see objects as partners, not as disposable toys.

Reuse beats single-use. Carry a bottle and a lunch container. Borrow or rent gear you need only for a weekend. Join or organize a swap at school for books and uniforms. Buy used when quality is high and safety is clear—helmets and safety gear should usually be new for protection, but many other items are safe to buy second-hand. Reuse does not mean you cannot enjoy new things; it means you do not buy new by default.

Cases show how habits change budgets and bins. In one case, your family switches from single-use paper towels to washable cloths for kitchen spills. After a small start-up cost, your trash shrinks and you save money each month. In another case, your club runs a uniform exchange at season's end. Parents are grateful, players look sharp, and fewer garments end up in the landfill. In a third case, you learn to maintain your bike—cleaning the chain, checking tire pressure, tightening bolts—and your transportation budget runs smoother all year.

Think about packaging. Many products ship in layers of plastic that add cost and waste. When you have a choice, pick the version with less packaging or a refill system. When you order online, group items to reduce trips. If a company offers packaging take-back, use it. Your decisions signal demand for better designs.

Energy use matters too. Devices that charge daily cost more to run than ones that sip power. Turn off lights when you leave, unplug chargers that are done, and use natural light when possible. If you cook, plan a few meals that use the oven once for multiple dishes. Small behaviors add up across weeks and families.

Finally, link sustainable spending to joy. Celebrate repairs with a photo. Name and appreciate the objects that serve you well for years. Share tips with friends without shaming. Money is a vote for the kind of world you want. When you vote for durability, repair, and reuse, your wallet and your planet both breathe easier.

## Chapter 28 — Level Up Your Earning: Skills, Resumes, References, and Interviews

More income starts with more value. Value comes from skills, reliability, and kindness. As a teen, you can grow all three faster than you think. This chapter shows you how to turn your effort into opportunities by presenting yourself clearly and practicing simple professional habits.

Begin with skills. Make a short list of tasks you can already do well and tasks you want to learn: tutoring a subject, basic coding, pet care, bike maintenance, baking, translation, organizing spaces, or running small events. Pick one to improve this month. Study a short tutorial, practice on your own, and ask for feedback from someone you trust. Skills are ladders; each rung makes the next job easier.

Create a one-page resume appropriate for your age. Include your name and contact information (with family approval), a short line about your goal, your skills, any volunteer work, and two references who have agreed to be contacted. Keep formatting clean and language specific. "Helped organize a neighborhood book swap; prepared flyers; sorted 300 books; managed check-in table." Specifics build trust.

References are people who can vouch for your reliability. Ask a coach, a teacher, a neighbor you helped, or a family friend. Confirm what they are comfortable saying. Thank them after someone calls. Protect your references by being choosy about which jobs you pursue; do not waste their time on projects you will not take seriously.

Interviews are structured conversations about fit. Prepare three points about why you want the job and how you can help. Practice a short story about a time you solved a problem or showed reliability. Arrive a few minutes early, dress simply and neatly, and bring a small notebook. Listen carefully, answer questions honestly, and ask one thoughtful question about the work. Afterward, send a short thank-you message that mentions something specific you discussed.

Cases reveal what works. In one case, you apply to be a counselor-in-training at a local camp. You highlight your experience organizing games for younger cousins and your first-aid mini course. You bring two references. You get the spot, show up early all summer, and leave with a strong recommendation for next year. In another case, you pitch a part-time job at a bike shop. You offer to start by cleaning and organizing on weekends and to learn basic repairs. The shop values your attitude and trains you. Your pay increases as your skills grow. In a third case, you do not get the job. You ask politely for one piece of feedback, learn that your answers were vague, and practice being specific. The next interview goes better.

Keep a simple portfolio of your work: photos, short descriptions, and notes about what you learned. When you apply for new opportunities, this portfolio becomes proof that you can deliver. Do not post private information or faces without permission. Treat your portfolio as a professional tool, not a social feed.

Finally, remember that money follows responsibility. Be the person who communicates early, who keeps their word, and who fixes small mistakes without drama. When you are consistent, adults trust you with bigger tasks and better pay. Leveling up is not a single leap. It is many small steps taken steadily.

## Chapter 29 — Education and Training Paths: Scholarships, Grants, and Smarter Choices

Education is an investment in your earning engine, and it comes in many forms: classes at school, community programs, apprenticeships, online courses, and future college or trade schools. The smartest path is the one that fits your interests, your budget, and your region's opportunities. This chapter helps you think about cost, value, and access so you can choose wisely.

Start by mapping your goals. Write three fields you enjoy and three skills you want to build. Talk to adults in those fields about what training actually helped them. Some careers require degrees; others reward certifications, portfolios, or hands-on practice. Knowing the difference prevents you from spending time and money on the wrong path.

Scholarships and grants are gifts you do not repay. Look locally first: civic groups, employers, unions, libraries, and community foundations often fund students for specific interests or service. Keep a simple spreadsheet of opportunities with deadlines, requirements, and contact info. Write applications in your own voice, show your work clearly, and ask a teacher to review. Apply for many small awards; several small wins can equal a big one.

Compare programs by total cost, not just tuition. Add fees, books, tools, travel, and the time you cannot work while you study. Some programs offer work-study options, paid internships, or part-time schedules. If two programs teach similar skills, choose the one that leaves you with less debt and more flexibility. Prestige is expensive; fit is priceless.

Cases demonstrate smart choices. In one case, you want to learn coding. A private boot camp costs more than you can afford. You start with free online courses, join your school's coding club, and build a small website for a local group. A mentor helps you apply for a summer scholarship at a community program. You arrive in the fall with a portfolio and no debt. In another case, you want to study culinary arts. You compare a faraway school with high living costs to a respected local program with strong restaurant partnerships. You pick local, work part-time in a kitchen, and graduate with experience and savings.

Guard against pressure tactics. If a school or program demands a commitment before you can compare options, step back. If a loan is presented as the only way, ask for other funding paths. Read contracts with an adult, and watch for refund policies and job placement claims that sound too perfect. Real programs welcome questions and transparency.

Learning never stops, and certificates can stack. Take a first step you can afford and a second step that builds on it. Use libraries and community centers as learning hubs. Teach someone what you learned; teaching locks skills in place. Your education plan is not a single decision at eighteen; it is a series of choices you remake as you grow.

Finally, remember that the goal is a life you want to live, not a label. Choose paths that match your values and allow you to contribute. Money matters, but meaning matters too. When both align, you will find energy to persist through the hard parts.

## Chapter 30 — Build Your Safety Net: Emergency Buffers and Bounce-  Back Plans

A safety net is money and habits that catch you when life yanks the floor. For teens, the net is small and simple: a tiny emergency buffer, a crisis budget plan, a list of helpers, and a habit of pausing before panic. The purpose is not to fear the future; it is to move through surprises with confidence.

Begin with a buffer. Set a modest target—perhaps the cost of one month of your typical flexible spending, or a fixed number like fifty to a hundred dollars depending on your life. This is not savings for fun goals; it is money that waits quietly for true needs: a bus pass when your bike breaks, a replacement charger for school, a copay at a clinic.

Keep the buffer in a safe, easily reachable place such as a bank savings account. Refill it after you use it. Think of it as a personal pit crew, ready between laps.

Write a crisis budget on a calm day. List the expenses you can pause quickly if needed: subscriptions, outings, upgrades. List the expenses you must protect: transport to school, basic meals, phone plan for safety. If income drops, you will not have energy to decide under stress. Your crisis budget makes decisions in advance. Share it with a caregiver so they can help you apply it if something happens.

Cases show the net in action. In one case, your laptop charger fails two days before a project is due. Instead of borrowing in a rush, you use the buffer to buy a replacement that same day and finish calmly. You then schedule a replacement buffer refill across two weeks. In another case, your parent's work hours are cut for a month. The family implements a temporary crisis plan: cooking from pantry staples, pausing entertainment subscriptions, and asking the phone provider for a short-term discount. Because you prepared, the month is tighter but not scary.

Make a helper list. Write down names and numbers of people you can call in specific situations—family, neighbors, a teacher, a counselor, a team coach. Add official numbers like your bank, your health clinic, and your school office. Store the list in your phone and on paper. In tough moments, brains forget. Lists remember for you.

Prevention belongs in your net. Maintain your gear, pack a small kit for days out, and charge devices overnight. Store a few shelf-stable meals at home if your family can. Learn basic first aid. Tiny habits reduce the number of emergencies you face. When fewer things go wrong, your buffer lasts longer.

Finally, pair your net with self-talk that steadies you. When a surprise hits, say, "Pause. Breathe. What is the next right step?" Use your plan, call a helper, and take the step. Then the next. Safety nets are built from money and from mindset. With both, you can bounce rather than break.

# DIRECTOR'S NOTES

# DIRECTOR'S NOTES